Jesus Loves the Little Children of the World

Jim Reimann
Illustrations by Julia Filipone-Erez

Jesus' disciples once came to Him to ask,
"Will you answer this hard question, and a truth unmask?
Who'll be the greatest when to heaven we go?"
So He stood a child before them—the answer to show.

He said, "You must become like this little child,"
Then with true loving care, Jesus Himself must have smiled.
"The greatest person must be humble and small,
In order to see the kingdom of heaven at all."

"And if you welcome a small child in My name,
You not only welcome the child, but Me just the same.
Yet if you cause a child to sin—I must warn:
You would be much better off, never to have been born."

Later children were brought to Jesus for prayer,
But His disciples scolded, "Get away from Him there!"
Yet Christ said, "Let the children come unto Me,
For heaven belongs to little ones like these, you see."

Then Jesus prayed for all the girls and the boys,
Blessing them all with His love, and with other great joys.
So if you are ever scared, lonely, or sad,
Go to Jesus in prayer, for He loves to make you glad.

Let's end today's story with this simple song,
For Jesus loves little children—to Him you belong.

Jesus loves the little children,
All the children of the world.
Red and yellow, black and white,
All are precious in His sight.
Jesus loves the little children of the world.

www.jesusbooks4kids

Rev. Jim Reimann
Israel Tour Leader of 25+ Pilgrimages
Editor of the Updated Editions of:
My Utmost for His Highest (Oswald Chambers)
Streams in the Desert (Lettie Cowman)
Morning by Morning (Charles Spurgeon)
Evening by Evening (Charles Spurgeon)

ISBN: 978-965-7607-03-9

For ordering information, please contact the publisher:

Intelecty, Ltd.
76 Hagalil
Nofit, Israel 36001
Tel: 97249930922
Fax: 972722830147
amirarkind@gmail.com

Printed in the Holy Land